Make your own Teddy Bear

Written by Brian and Donna Gibbs

KUDOS

Published by Kudos, an imprint of Top That! Publishing plc.
Copyright © 2005 Top That! Publishing plc,
Tide Mill Way, Woodbridge, Suffolk, IP12 IAP, UK
www.kudosbooks.com
Kudos is a Trademark of Top That! Publishing plc

Contents

Introduction

For over a hundred years, the teddy bear has been a popular toy, loved and cherished by children throughout the world. What's more, it is the one childhood toy that many carry into adulthood as a reminder of their younger days.

By following the step-by-step guide in this book you will be able to complete your very own teddy bear in the traditional style. Whether it is for you or to be offered as a gift, the finished teddy will provide endless hours of pleasure to its owner.

After learning the basic techniques necessary for this project you're sure to have the confidence and desire to create teddy bears of your own design in the future.

The book also includes an insight into the teddy bear's evolution and there are hints and tips on collecting them.

History of the Teddy Bear

President Theodore Roosevelt

One of the most enduringly popular toys of recent history, the first teddy bear is thought to have been made somewhere around 1902. Unfortunately, there is no conclusive documentary evidence to support the arguments of either of the manufacturers claiming to have made the first one.

It is generally accepted that the idea of the teddy was a result of President Theodore Roosevelt refusing to shoot a bear cub whilst on a hunting trip, an event quickly seized upon by the press.

A famous cartoon drawn by Clifford Berryman appeared in the Washington Post in November 1902. Entitled 'Drawing the line in Mississippi' the cartoon showed the president turning his back on a captive bear cub. The bear cub began to appear in other cartoons which Berryman drew throughout Theodore Roosevelt's career and so the association began.

This caught the attention of Morris Michtom, a Russian immigrant who owned a store in Brooklyn selling sweets, novelties and toys.

And so a craze began: Just one of many cartoons by Clifford Berryman, featuring Theodore Roosevelt and a bear.

History of the Teddy Bear

A Roosevelt teddy bear

Michtom decided to make a small, soft toy bear cub, with movable arms and legs, from brown plush fabric. He then displayed the prototype in the shop window alongside a newspaper clipping of the cartoon. This aroused so much interest that he decided to market the idea.

He wrote to the president asking permission to call the toy 'Teddy's Bear' and was astounded to receive a reply written in the president's own hand (unusual even in those days) which read, "I don't think my name is worth much to the toy bear business but you are welcome to use it."

Michtom made a sample of the bear and sent one to the president and another to the buyer of a large toy wholesaler, Butler Bros, who not only agreed to take the entire output of the bears but also to guarantee credit for the fabric needed for their manufacture.

This was the birth of a company called The Ideal Novelty and Toy Company, later renamed as The Ideal Toy Company. If the president's letter could be found this would prove the American claim to the honour of inventing the teddy bear.

However, there is another contender for the title: the German toy manufacturer Margarete Steiff.

Steiff was already a well-established maker of felt toys. Her products, mainly domestic and farm animals were proving to be very popular and the business was thriving with worldwide exports.

Margarete's nephew, Richard Fritz, was an art student who spent his spare time perfecting his painting and drawing. During 1902 he made several visits to the zoo at Stuttgart, sketching the animals including the bears.

While studying his drawings, it occurred to him that he might try to design a bear toy that would be more cuddly and realistic than the felt toys that his aunt was producing.

The young artist soon produced a small bear with a movable head and joints from a fluffy mohair fabric. His aunt was initially unenthusiastic but she allowed the toy to be marketed in America to see if there was any enthusiasm for it.

A pair of Steiff bears dating back to 1908

History of the Teddy Bear

An extremely rare, dark blue Steiff bear circa 1909

Margarete was not in the least surprised when the bear failed to inspire the agents and that no orders for the new toy materialised. Richard was disappointed but, undaunted, he took his creation to a toy fair in Leipzig in 1903.

Initially there was little interest in his design but at the end of the last day of the fair, when all of the exhibits were being packed away, Richard was engaged in conversation by Hermann Berg from the New York wholesalers Geo Borgfeldt and Co. Berg remarked that he had found the fair rather dull and that the felt toys on show were uninspiring. At this point Richard revealed his cuddly bear to Hermann who immediately exclaimed that this was exactly what he was looking for and placed an initial order for 3,000 bears.

While it is impossible to substantiate the merits of either claim, what is clear is that both companies went from strength to strength on the back of the teddy bear. Indeed, the Steiff factory had to expand three times between 1903 and 1908. After the death of Margarete Steiff in 1909, her company continued to expand with outlets all over the world and this company is still making teddy bears today.

Around this period, teddy bear manufacture also began in England. A company that made tea cosies and pincushions called J.K. Farnell and Company started to design and make bears and continued to do so until it closed in 1968.

During both World Wars teddy bear production ceased with many well-known teddy bear manufacturers diversifying into war work such as munitions and the production of life jackets.

It wasn't until the 1950s that teddy-bear making was re-established, with new materials introduced. Synthetic plush and plastics soon evolved to allow for improvements in the quality of children's toys and safety eyes, noses and joints became an industry standard.

A late 1940s bear

Teddy Bear Timeline

Steiff's 1912 black teddy bear

Take a brief journey through time and discover a few interesting events in the history of the teddy bear.

1834 *Goldilocks and the Three Bears* is written by Robert Southey.

c. 1897 Toy bears featured in Steiff catalogue for the first time.

1899 Margarete Steiff registers patents for soft toy designs including a dancing bear.

1902 Morris Michtom sells the first 'Teddy's Bear' in his Brooklyn shop.

1903 Steiff Company sells 3,000 units of a toy bear to America.

1906 First advertisement using the words Teddy Bear appears.

1908 First British teddy bears made by J.K. Farnell.

1912 Steiff Company creates black teddy bears. They are intended as mourning gifts after the sinking of the Titanic.

1919 Pioneers Alcock and Brown take teddy bears on the first-ever non-stop Atlantic flight.

1920 First Rupert Bear picture story appears in the UK newspaper, the *Daily Express*.

1926 *Winnie-the-Pooh* by A.A. Milne is published for the first time.

1938 Royal warrant granted to British teddy bear makers Chad Valley.

1952 Teddy bear glove puppet Sooty debuts on British television.

1958 The first Paddington story, *A Bear Called Paddington*, written by Michael Bond, is published.

1975 Walt Disney's first animated film of *Winnie-the-Pooh* appears.

1985 Christie's of London hold the first ever teddy bear only auction.

1989 Happy, a 1926 mohaired-tipped Steiff bear, is sold at auction in London for £55,000.

1994 Teddy Girl, a 1904 cinnamon Steiff bear is sold at auction in London for £110,000.

1998 The 8.5 mm bear called Guinness is accepted by *The Guinness Book of Records* as the world's smallest teddy bear.

Sooty and friends, glove puppets

Walt Disney's Winnie-the-Pooh

Teddy Bear Trivia

Goldilocks

A teddy bear's picnic

Goldilocks

Robert Southey, the author of *Goldilocks and the Three Bears*, began making his mark when he was expelled from Westminster School for writing an essay objecting to flogging.

As a young man he met the poet Samuel Taylor Coleridge and the two became close friends, writing a play together and eventually marrying two sisters.

Southey became well known for his poems such as 'Joan of Arc' and 'The Battle of Blenheim' and in 1813 was appointed Poet Laureate, the greatest honour available to a British poet. In 1835 he was awarded a £300 pension by Robert Peel, Britain's prime minister at the time and the founder of the first police force.

The Teddy Bear's Picnic

The music of the famous song, *The Teddy Bear's Picnic*, was written by American composer J.K. Bratton in 1907. At this time it was called *The Teddy Bear Two Step*. The lyrics were added in 1930 by Irishman Jimmy Kennedy, a tremendously successful songwriter who achieved around 200 worldwide hits. His other records include *Istanbul not Constantinople* and wartime classic *Hang Out Your Washing on the Siegfried Line*.

Smokey Bear

In 1944 Smokey Bear was adopted as the mascot of the United States Forest Fire Prevention Campaign. He is now part of the longest-running public service advertising campaign in the US. When a real bear was caught up in a forest fire in New Mexico it led to him becoming the living symbol of Smokey.

This bear cub climbed a tree to try to avoid the blaze, but when the fire had passed through the forest the bear was badly burnt. His rescue caught the public imagination and, after the cub had received medical treatment, he was housed in the National Zoo in Washington DC.

Buttons

The eyes of early teddy bears were made of shoe buttons. Boots and shoes were once fastened with small, black, half-domed buttons that made perfect-looking eyes.

Smokey Bear

Shoe buttons were often used for eyes

Teddy Bear Trivia

Biffo the Bear

Biffo the Bear

British comic strip favourite Biffo the Bear appeared on the cover of *The Beano* for the first time in 1948. He replaced Eggo the Ostrich who had been there since the comic strip's inception ten years before.

Good Bears of the World

The charity Good Bears of the World was founded in England by Jim Ownby in 1969. Its stated aim is to provide teddy bears to children of all ages where love, solace and comfort can make a difference. In 2003 the charity gave away over 20,000 teddy bears.

Great Teddy Bear Rally

In 1979 famous English aristocrat the Marquis of Bath organised the Great Teddy Bear Rally. Over 15,000 people and around 2,000 teddy bears congregated at his stately home, Longleat, in order to raise money for charity. In Amherst, Massachusetts, the 21st Annual Teddy Bear Rally took place on 6th August, 2004 and drew a crowd of 20,000 people. Visitors enjoyed Winnie-the-Pooh readings, a parade, a used bear lot and a teddy bear hospital.

Special Day

In the US there is not one but two teddy bear days. There is National Teddy Bear Day, which is celebrated on 9th September, and National American Teddy Bear Day on 14th November.

Colours

Most teddy bears are dark brown, light brown or yellow in colour. Black, white, grey and dark red bears are much rarer and, therefore, more valuable.

Fancy Dress

Teddy bears have become so popular over the past twenty years that, in America and Japan, they are put in shows, dressed in specially made clothes that make them look like famous people (kings and queens, film and book characters etc).

Teddy Bear Museum

In 1988 Gyles and Michele Brandreth opened the Teddy Bear Museum in Stratford-upon-Avon. Gyles is a former Tory MP and a regular contributor to British television and radio panel shows. There are also many more teddy bear museums around the world.

A Queen Mother teddy bear

Collecting Teddy Bears

'Artist bears'

Teddy bears are one of the most popular things for people to collect. In fact, there is a word that describes those who have a penchant for the humble teddy bear: 'arctophile' (in Greek 'arctos' is the word for bear and 'philos' the word for love). Many arctophiles collect not only teddy bears but also related paraphernalia such as key rings and tee shirts. Incidentally, a collection of teddy bears is known as a 'hug'!

Teddy bears are collected for a number of reasons: nostalgia for the hazily remembered years of childhood; financial investment; or just because of an affection for the style or charm of one particular manufacturer or 'artist bear'.

'Artist bear' is the term used to describe a teddy bear that has been designed, created and finished by an individual bear maker who has interpreted the traditional teddy bear in their own way. Often these bears will only be made in very limited editions, with their rarity making them highly collectable.

By the end of the twentieth century, bear collecting had become a serious pastime for many people. While it doesn't necessarily have to be an expensive hobby, some particularly rare and desirable teddy bears have sold for astonishing sums. For example, in 1989, an original Steiff bear called Happy was sold at auction for a staggering £55,000.

Collecting is easily personalised to suit your pocket. It can give great pleasure and of course your knowledge will increase as your collection grows. This is because you will want to find out as much as possible about each acquisition, such as the manufacturer, the age, the value etc.

All this information can be gleaned from books, the internet or simply by talking to the person selling the bear. Your increased knowledge will make the enjoyment of each addition to your collection all the more pleasurable.

Friends will ask questions and, of course, with your new-found knowledge, you will soon become quite an expert on the subject and never tire of telling them the full history of any bear in your possession.

A 'hug' of bears

Collecting Teddy Bears

Ty Beanie bears

A special edition teddy honouring the second World War

Bear collecting need not take over the whole house. In fact, if space is an issue then why not specialise in miniature teddies? There are teddy bears available in all sizes, from the ultra small, that will sit easily in the palm of your hand, to almost life size. Most collectors tend to specialise in a particular style or manufacturer. Whatever your decision, the important thing is that you like what you are collecting. As with fine arts and antiques, it is far better to invest in something you really like rather than invest in something because of its financial potential.

If collecting bears is something that appeals to you then the first thing to do is to decide on your preferred style of teddy. You may wish to specialise in one particular type of bear, such as the Beanie, or you may prefer to collect a range of teddy bears from the earliest antique models right up to present-day designs.

Whatever your choice, you will have plenty of scope as there are a great many teddy bears to be found of all shapes, sizes, styles and prices. Generally speaking, the older your bear the more valuable it will be but, of course, this works two ways. High cost may well be a factor in deciding whether to buy or not. Bears from the 1950s and later are usually fairly reasonably priced as there are a great many good examples still around.

A special millennium edition
Ty Beanie bear

Collecting Teddy Bears

A Steiff bear

Hermann Bears

It is well worth keeping your eyes open for that little gem at market stalls, car boot sales or in charity shops. The recent spate of television programmes on collectables has made bargains harder to find, but there are still some out there.

It is worth recording all the important details of your bears, such as age, manufacturer and dimensions. Photograph each bear from several angles as this will help greatly if you need expert advice to establish the type of bear that you have. This will not only help to identify your bear, but if there is any great value to the bear, the information will be helpful for insurance purposes.

As a basic guide, early Steiff bears are the most collectable. The next most sought after are early Ideal American bears. These have tubby bodies, triangular faces and long, straight arms and legs. Novelty bears from this time such as the 1907 Laughing Roosevelt Bear, which opens its mouth to display large teeth, and the 1917 red, white and blue Patriotic Bear with electric light bulb eyes are also highly collectable.

If you're after early European bears look out for those manufactured by German firms Bing, Schuco and Hermann. For British bears seek out JK Farrell, Dean's and Merrrythought versions.

It wasn't really until the 1970s that the teddy bear collectors' market developed. Before this few people had suspected that teddy bears would become so valuable. Now that the demand for ancient bears exceeds supply some amazing prices are being achieved.

Steiff made many famous bears and here are a few, most of which have had replicas produced of them since 1980:

1907 Hot Water Bottle Bear: only ninety were produced. A metal hot water bottle was concealed in the bear's tummy; the opening closed by strong ribbon lacing around hooks.

1908-17 Muzzle Bears: produced in white and light to dark brown in ten different sizes.

1910-18 Pantom Bear: attached to six wires, just over 6000 produced in two sizes.

1912 Mourning Bear: in memory of the Titanic disaster. One such bear, in excellent condition, fetched £80,000 at an auction at Christies in December 2000.

1929-50 Teddy Baby: produced in twelve sizes and made in mohair, artificial and wool plush. Mainly produced in dark brown or creamy coloured mohair but some were white and these are now very collectable.

1930-36 Dicky Bear: made in white or blond with a brown stitched nose, or gold with black stitched nose. Characterised by a smiling mouth.

1951 onwards Zotty Bears: mainly caramel coloured mohair tipped with white. There was also a Sleeping or Floppy Zotty, positioned lying down with closed eyes.

Dean's Bears

Merrythought Bears

Recognising Different Manufacturers

A classic Steiff bear

While all teddy bears are designed both to appeal to the customer and to be easy to produce, over the years teddy bear manufacturers have developed their own individual styles. This has enabled enthusiasts to identify a particular manufacturer. However, there are so many teddy bears around that to become an expert takes years of experience.

If you want to spot a 1950s teddy bear, there are a number of clues to look for. Although the war had finished, materials were still relatively scarce. To overcome this, designers compromised by using cheaper alternatives such as vegetable fibre for the fabric material, and some well-known teddy bear makers even used nettles as a basis! Another telltale sign of 1950s bears is that they were often re-designed with much shorter arms and legs, allowing manufacturers to save on material costs.

One of the best-known manufacturers in the teddy bear world is Steiff. These are the teddy bears that so often make the headlines all over the world with record-breaking prices at famous auctions. If you are lucky, identification of a genuine Steiff can be quite easy because all of their teddies have an exclusive trait of a 'button' in the ear. This is still used today by Steiff and is simply a metal button rivetted in one of the teddy's ears. Sometimes it is missing, either because of extreme abuse by the child, or, most commonly, because it has been removed by a concerned parent worried their child may ingest the button should it ever work loose. Even so, if you look hard enough it is usually possible to see evidence of where the button was originally fitted.

Even the way a bear is sewn up will give away vital clues. For instance, Steiff used to assemble the teddy bear as a unit and then stuff the arms and legs in situ. This meant that the final closing seam on each limb was still visible to the more eagle eyed. If you look closely at the arm and leg joints, you may well see that hand stitching has been used to close the seam at the top of each limb around the joint disc areas.

Another clue to a Steiff design is in the closing of the final seam on the bear's body, which, unusually is made on the front of the bear. Most manufacturers used to fill the bear through the back and then close the seam that runs

A Steiff bear's 'button' ear tag

Stuffing the limbs of a Steiff bear in situ

Recognising Different Manufacturers

A selection of manufacturer's hallmarks

vertically down the centre back seam. Other than Steiff only one manufacturer deviated from this method and that was Bing, another German bear maker. Next time you see an old bear for sale at a bargain price, look more closely at these details. That way hopefully you will notice if it turns out you are holding a valuable teddy bear!

Both Schuco and Bing made some wonderful mechanical bears during the interwar years. These included bears that could walk, dance and even perform somersaults. You will be very lucky indeed to see one of these available at less than market value.

If you just want to collect teddy bears with no special value you will find that you are not alone. In the US alone in 1999 over $400 million was spent on teddy bears.

A very rare Bing walking teddy bear
circa 1910

Famous Bears

Teddy Girl

In the last hundred years some teddy bears have become household names. A few of these bears were mascots but many were the inspiration behind television programmes, films and books that have enthralled children everywhere.

Teddy Girl

Teddy Girl was an early Steiff creation, made in 1904. This much sought-after teddy bear hit the television news networks in December 1994 when Mr Yoshi Sekiguchi bought Teddy Girl (still in pristine condition) at auction for a staggering world record price of £110,000.

Rupert

Rupert the Bear began life as a cartoon strip in the *Daily Express* newspaper on 8th November, 1920. In 1935, the editor of the paper decided that they had enough of the cartoon strips to produce an annual so in that year the first Rupert annual was launched.

Rupert

Famous Bears

A Winnie-the-Pooh from the 1980s

The current Winnie-the-Pooh style

During the Second World War Rupert was the only newspaper picture strip that was allowed to continue publication. It was so popular that the government thought it would dent the public's morale if it was stopped.

The Rupert annual is as popular today as it was all those years ago and still ranks in the top three most popular children's annuals every year.

Winnie-the-Pooh

Winnie-the-Pooh was created by A.A. Milne over seventy years ago and was associated with his poem, *Christopher Robin*, written for his son. The first published book appeared in October 1926 and the beautiful illustrations by E.H. Shepard helped to make the stories more magical for the readers.

Further stories were written and it is now estimated that worldwide book sales stand at over 20 million copies! It was later immortalised as a popular cartoon by the Walt Disney studio, who also sell replica Winnies, complete with red tops. Today Pooh has spread his influence even further with such novelty books as *The Tao of Pooh* and *The Te of Piglet*.

Aloysius

Aloysius, the bear in Evelyn Waugh's *Brideshead Revisited*, was brought into the public consciousness by the television series in the 1980s. Replicas of this bear are still sought after today and were possibly responsible for the huge resurgence of teddy bear interest at that time.

Sooty

In 1948 Harry Corbett, an amateur magician, paid 7/6d (37.5 new pence) for a glove puppet from a stall in Blackpool to amuse his children. A few years later in the early 1950s he appeared on British television with a glove puppet bear made from gold mohair with black ears. This bear was called Sooty and was set to entertain generations of children.

Pooky

Pooky is the teddy bear Garfield the cat, creation of American cartoonist Jim Davis, and found in a drawer. The cartoon strip began in June 1978 and has become the most widely read cartoon of all time. Currently, the Garfield cartoon appears in over 2,500 different newspapers around the world every day. So, in terms of numbers, Pooky is the world's best known teddy bear ever!

Sooty

Pooky

Famous Bears

Paddington

Paddington

Michael Bond, a cameraman working for the BBC in London, was returning home rather late one Christmas Eve in the mid 1950s and, at the last minute, purchased a rather forlorn looking teddy bear as a present for his wife. As they lived quite near Paddington station at the time they called the bear Paddington. Soon afterwards Michael decided to write a children's story about a bear.

Within ten days he felt that he had enough material for a book. He contacted his agent who decided it would indeed make a good children's story and lo and behold the book *A Bear called Paddington* was born. Thirty million copies of Paddington books have now been sold and there have been hundreds of television programmes based on the characterful bear.

Yogi Bear

Yogi Bear is one of the most popular Hanna-Barbera stars of all time, rivalled only by *The Flintstones* and *Scooby-Doo*. He was first seen in 1958 on the back of the Huckleberry Hound Show, but was given his own show in 1961. The cartoon bear lives in Jellystone National

Park with his sidekick Boo Boo, who serves as Yogi's conscience. His adventures mainly centre on his attempts to steal picnic baskets and his ability to confound Ranger Smith.

Fozzie Bear

Fozzie Bear is one of the stars of Jim Henson's popular *Muppet Show*, which first aired in 1976. A comical fuzzy brown bear, he just wants to be the world's funniest comedian. Unfortunately his jokes are terrible and consequently, he is constantly heckled by Statler and Waldorf, the two old critics in the audience. Fozzie's name derives from Frank Oz, the muppeteer who played and voiced the bear's character.

Bear in the Big Blue House

This popular Jim Henson creation first hit the airwaves in 1998. In the show, the cuddly and caring Bear teaches and explores through the lessons of each episode. With help from his friends Luna, Tutter, Shadow, Pip and Pop, Treelo, and Ojo, Bear takes preschoolers into a world of imagination where they learn new things like music, dancing and colours. He'll even do the Bear Cha Cha Cha!

Fozzie Bear

Famous Bears

Little Bear

A Care Bear

Little Bear

The Little Bear books, illustrated by Maurice Sendak and written by Else Holmelund Minarik, were first published in 1957 and were instantly popular. The stories are about the spirited adventures of a curious, young cub and his animal friends. In 1995, these wonderful characters reached an even wider audience when the animated series was first shown.

Care Bears

The Care Bears began life in 1981 as greetings card characters but soon became best-selling soft toys. The *Care Bear Movie* of 1985 was such a success, it spawned sequels in 1986 and 1987.

The Care Bears didn't wear their hearts on their sleeve – but on their stomachs! Each Care Bear wears a symbol representing a feeling. They lived in the land of Care-A-Lot from where they looked for children who needed help on earth.

Baloo the Bear

Baloo the bear first made his appearance in Rudyard Kipling's collection of stories, published as The Jungle Book in 1894. However, he was immortalised when Disney adapted the story in their 1967 film of the same name. Baloo is one of Mowgli's true friends, dedicated to helping him be happy – and bringing with him a great sense of rhythm and style.

Baloo with Mowgli

Famous Owners

Prince Charles

Teddy bear love affairs are not just reserved for children; adults love them too. Here are just a few famous fans of the cuddly toy.

Royal Teddies

When Prince Charles was a little boy, he had a special teddy who went with him to school. His father, Prince Philip, had a favourite toy bear too. This bear is now on show at the Teddy Bear Museum in Stratford-upon-Avon. Also in the museum is Percy, who belonged to Henry Thynne, the sixth Marquess of Bath and creator of Longleat Safari Park.

World-renowned romantic novelist and relative of Princess Diana, Barbara Cartland was the proud owner of a colourful bear called The Prince Of Love.

Alcock and Brown

Captain John Alcock and Lieutenant Arthur Whitten Brown made the first non-stop crossing of the Atlantic in 1919, but they didn't do it without some help from their teddies! They took off in their modified Vickers Vimy from Newfoundland and landed in Clifden in Ireland sixteen hours and twenty seven minutes later. The teddy bear mascots they took with them certainly worked their magic.

Donald Campbell

Donald Campbell had a mascot teddy bear called Mr Whoppit, who sported a bluebird motif on his waistcoat. In 1967, Mr Whoppit was in the cockpit at the time of Campbell's fatal attempt on the world water speed record at Coniston Water in the Lake District.

After the crash there was very little left of the speedboat, but the bear was found. Being filled with Kapok, it floated to the surface shortly after the accident. Replicas of this bear were made by the British teddy bear maker Merrythought in 1992.

Elvis Presley

Elvis Presley, the king of rock 'n' roll, was known to be very keen on teddies. Indeed, he had a big hit in 1957 with a song called 'Teddy Bear'.

Margot Fonteyn

Dame Margot Fonteyn, one of the greatest ballet dancers of all time, travelled everywhere with her childhood bear.

Mr Whoppit

Getting Started

With the kit that accompanies this book you can make your very own teddy bear. The kit contains: light fur-type material; dark brown material for the paws; stuffing; thread; the teddy bear's eyes and nose; arm and leg joints; a length of ribbon; and the pattern. You will also need the following:

Scissors

Make sure you use good quality, sharp dressmaker's scissors. These will help you keep the pattern accurate and will also enable you to cut the fabric successfully. It's a good idea to keep dressmaking scissors separate and not use them for kitchen chores or any other purpose.

Pins

It is advisable to use strong, extra-long pins with glass heads. You will need strong pins because of the thickness of the fabrics you are using.

Needles

Either dressmaker's hand needles or machine needles will do. When sewing on the bear's nose you may find it a good idea to use an embroidery needle with a large eye.

Thread

Should you require more thread, use six-stranded embroidery thread. This will be strong enough for stitching the eyes, ears and head.

Thimble

You will find this useful when working with strong fabrics. *Tip*: wet your finger before placing the thimble over it to prevent movement.

Marker Pen

Use a marker pen or dressmaker's chalk to mark positions for holes and joints.

Awl

Use an awl or knitting needle to push through the fabric where the joints are positioned, to make a hole without cutting.

Preparing the Stuffing

There are a number of different types of stuffing available. The variety supplied in this pack needs to be carefully teased to plump it out until it has the appearance and density of candyfloss.

Using the Pattern

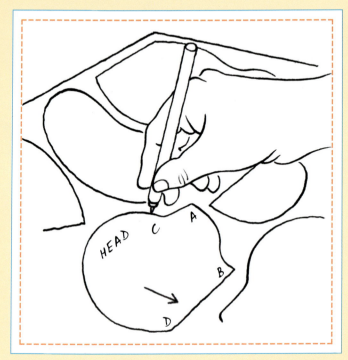

Marking the fabric

Now it's time to begin making your very own bear. It is best to read all the instructions through thoroughly before you begin. That way you are less likely to make any mistakes. If you like you can photocopy the pattern supplied – that way you can use it again to make other bears.

Making Card Templates

Card is more durable than paper and easier to draw around. Roughly cut out all of the paper pattern pieces and paste them onto thin card. Carefully cut each one out, then use a sharp pointed tool, such as an awl or a knitting needle, to make small holes at the joint and eye positions as well as the arm and leg positions on the body. Also mark the points that indicate where the openings are to be, as all of this information will need to be transferred to the fabric at the next stage.

Marking The Fabric

Before the templates are positioned on the back of the fabric it is important to notice which way the pile is lying. Stroke the fur to find which way feels smoothest; the direction you would stroke an animal. This is the direction the pile is lying and all of the templates need to be placed on the back of the fabric with the arrows following this direction.

To help you remember the pile direction it is a good idea to draw an arrow on the back of the fabric for reference.

Placing Card Templates

Place all the card templates that need to be cut from the fur onto the back of the fabric as close together as possible so that the minimal amount of fur is wasted. Then, once you are sure they all fit, and with the pile in the right direction, draw around each piece with a permanent marker pen remembering to transfer all of the important information such as joint and eye positions as well as the openings for turning and stuffing the bear.

The same can now be done with the felt and the foot and paw pad templates. The only difference with the procedure is that felt does not have a pile direction and so the direction that you place the pieces is not so critical.

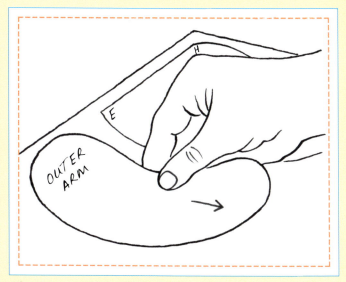

Placing card template

Using the Pattern

Cutting out

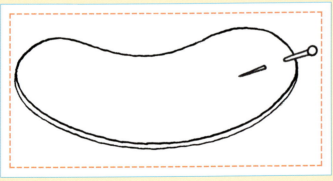

Pinning

Cutting Out

Take great care when cutting out pieces from the fur fabric. If you just chop the pieces out it is very likely that you will cut away most of the fur pile as you go, leaving you short of material!

The correct way to cut any pile fabric is to slide the lower blade of the scissors through the pile so it is directly touching the fabric backing. Snip the backing, then slide the point of the scissors forward and snip again.

It really is worthwhile taking your time when cutting out the pieces as effort now will help you make a far better bear.

Pinning

When two pieces are ready to be stitched the first step is to pin them together. The pieces should be placed right sides together, making sure that the outer edges line up without stretching the fabric. Insert the first pin at the top of the piece with the point facing inwards (this ensures the pins pierce only the fabric and not your fingers).

Before inserting the next pin use the point to tuck the fur to the inside so that it will not be trapped in the seam when it is sewn. Continue adding pins at around 2 cm intervals, tucking in the fur as you go, until the pieces are held securely together.

There are only a few basic stitching techniques that you need to know. All of them are easy to master and once learned they can be used time after time.

Oversewing

When two pieces of pile fabric are placed right sides together they have a tendency to 'walk' as one piece slides and pushes against the other. To make sewing the pieces together easier after pinning they should have the edges oversewn together to hold them in place.

Thread your needle and knot the thread at one end. From the back of the fabric, pass the needle through both layers to the front and pull the thread through. Take the needle to the back of the fabric and pass through both layers again to emerge at the front. This will leave a loop of thread holding the edges of the fabric together.

Continue in this way, inserting the needle at the back of the fabric and pulling through to the front, sewing all around the edges of the fabric so that the pieces are securely held together. Remember to leave the openings as marked on the pattern.

Oversewing has one other advantage; if the fabric you are using has a tendency to fray, the stitches will help prevent this from happening.

Stitching Techniques

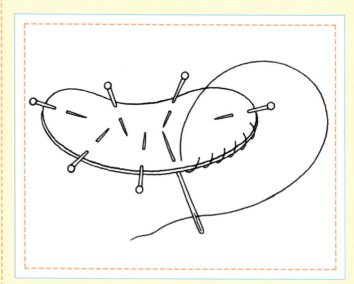

Oversewing

Stitching Techniques

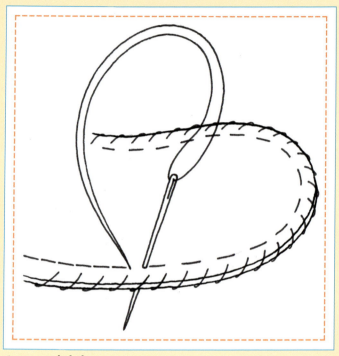

Seam stitching

Seam Stitching

The pattern has a 6 mm seam allowance included so this is how far away from the edge of the fabric your stitching should be.

For machine stitching, use a medium-length stitch and sew each seam twice for added strength. If hand stitching, use a double length of thread and knot the end. Pass the needle through the fabric from the back to the front and pull the thread through. Then re-insert the needle from the front to the back about 3 mm away. From the back make another 3 mm stitch and continue in this way until you have completed the seam.

Once the end of the seam has been reached it needs to be reinforced and made stronger to cope with the demands of everyday child's play so reverse the direction of your stitching and carry on making these small stitches in between the ones already made.

This method is similar to backstitching but it is easier to achieve a neater finish and gives a strong seam equal to a machine-stitched seam.

Ladder Stitch

This very useful stitch is used for attaching the ears and to close the final seams in the arms, legs and body after they have been jointed and stuffed.

Thread your needle with a double length of thread and knot one end. Insert the needle to one side of the top of the opening from the inside and pull the thread through so that the knot is hidden inside. Take the needle over to the other side of the opening, re-insert it directly opposite the thread and make a small stitch.

As the thread is pulled the edges of the opening will be pulled together. If the stitches are not placed directly opposite each other the fabric will pucker when the thread is pulled so take time to place the stitches carefully.

Continue to make a series of small stitches alternately on each side of the opening, like the rungs of a ladder, until you reach the bottom.

Ladder stitch

Making the Bear

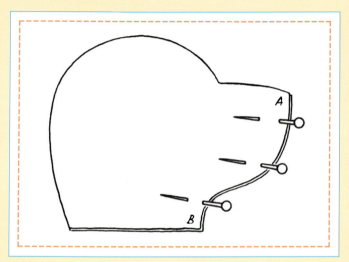

Step 1

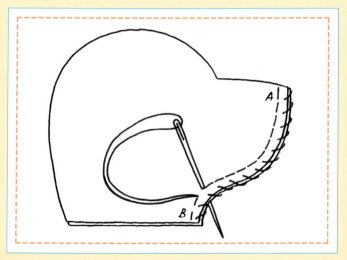

Step 2

Head

The head is made in two stages and is worth taking time over, as this is the most noticeable part of the finished bear.

1. Place the two head pieces furry sides together and pin along the front curved seam from point A to point B.

Leave the rest of the head unpinned as this will be sewn together during the next stage (we are only dealing with this front seam at this point).

2. Oversew along this front seam to hold it securely in place ready for seam stitching and then remove all of the pins.

Starting at the top of the seam, carefully stitch down the front curved edge from point A to B carefully following the 6 mm seam allowance.

3. Now the head gusset can be inserted. This is probably the trickiest part of making any teddy bear but it is not really that difficult.

Take the head gusset and pin it to the head with the right sides together at the tip of the nose (point A). Tuck the fur to the inside with your pins as you work, then insert the next pins at points C, which are on both sides of the head gusset near to the eye positions.

Finally, place the next two pins at both points marked D. Once the head gusset is held securely at these key points you can continue to add more pins all around the edges and between the pins to secure it in place. However, the bottom straight edge must be left open so that the head can be attached to the body a little later.

4. Take your needle and thread and oversew the head gusset to the head to hold it in place ready for stitching. Carefully follow the 6 mm seam allowance and stitch the head gusset in place, taking particular care around the tip of the nose. It is very easy to pucker the fabric in this area, especially if you are using a sewing machine. Sew slowly on the machine to prevent this.

If the fabric does become puckered it can lead to an off-centre nose, which will be very noticeable. If you find you have this problem it is well worth spending a few minutes to unpick the stitches and sew the seam again to achieve a smoother finish.

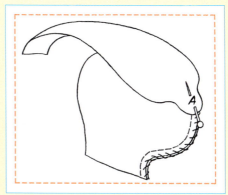

Step 3

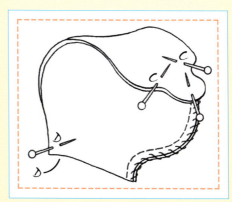

The second point D is on the other side of the head

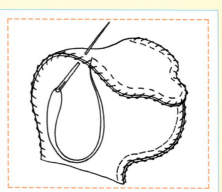

Step 4

Making the Bear

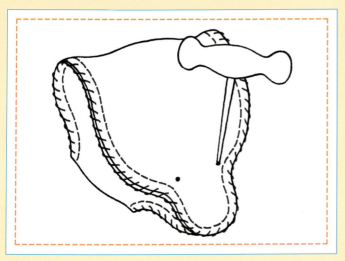

Step 5

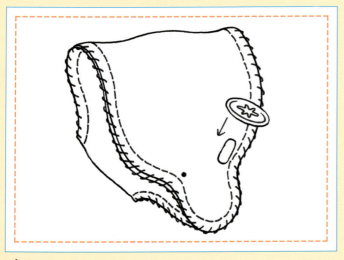

Step 6

5. Do not turn the head the right way out yet because the eyes have to be attached first. If you try to add the eyes later it may become difficult to reach inside the head to attach the washers. It's better to do it with the head still the wrong way out, as it is easier to find the marks to indicate the eye positions.

Make small holes with a sharp tool, such as an awl or knitting needle, at the eye position points marked on the pattern. Do not be tempted to use scissors to cut a hole, as this will make the holes too big and you may be in danger of the eye passing all the way through the fabric.

An awl or knitting needle will gently part the threads of the fabric rather then slice through them and so stretching or fraying should not be a problem.

6. From the right side (which at the moment is inside the head) push the stem of the eye through the hole. Place the washer on to the eye stem and push down firmly. These washers are quite a tight fit and you may find it a little difficult at first.

If you are having trouble pushing the washer onto the stem of the eye, or it is not level as you push down, try using a thimble placed over the stem to push down on. Do the same with the other eye, then check to make sure that there is no possibility of either eye coming loose.

7. Once the eyes are securely in place the nose can be attached. Make a small hole with your awl or knitting needle at point A. It is better to make the hole slightly to one side of the seam rather than break through the stitching.

From the right side of the head (inside) push the stem of the nose through the hole and attach the washer securely, checking to see that it is firmly in place before finally turning the head right side out.

8. Making the ears has to be the easiest part of making a teddy bear! Place two ear pieces right sides together and pin to hold in position. Oversew around the curved edge only, leaving the bottom straight edge open to allow the ear to be turned right side out. Remove the pins and stitch around the curved edge only, again leaving the bottom straight edge open.

9. Turn the ear right side out and tuck the raw edges of the straight edge to the inside. Take a needle and a double length of thread and ladder stitch the opening to close. Repeat with the other ear.

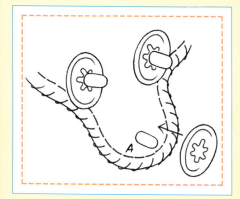

Step 7

Step 8

Step 9

Making the Bear

Step 1

Step 2

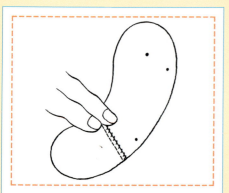

Step 3

Arms

There are three pieces that make up each arm: an inner arm, an outer arm and a paw pad.

1. First of all the paw pad has to be attached to the inner arm. Matching points M and N on the straight edges of the inner arm and the paw pad, place a felt paw pad on top of an inner arm, keeping the straight edges level. Pin the pad in place, tucking the fur pile to the inside as you go.

2. Oversew along the straight edge and remove the pins. Now stitch across the straight edge 6 mm from the edge of the fabric.

3. Unfold the paw pad to show the completed arm shape, pressing the seam upwards towards the top of the arm with your fingers.

4. Place this completed inner arm on top of the corresponding outer arm, right side in, and pin in place. Start by placing the first pin at the top of the arm, then place the second pin at the bottom of the paw pad. Check to make sure that the fabric edges will all line up and continue to pin all around the arm.

5. Oversew the edges together to hold them securely in place, remembering to leave the opening as marked on the pattern for turning and stuffing, then remove the pins.

Stitch the arm pieces together, leaving the opening as marked on the pattern and then turn the arm right side out. Make sure you tuck in the pile as you sew!

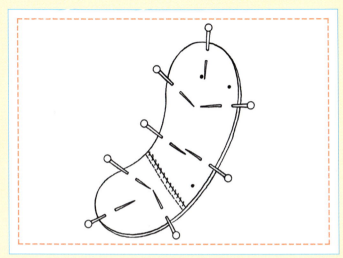

Step 4

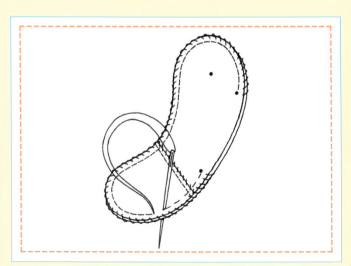

Step 5

Making the Bear

Step 6

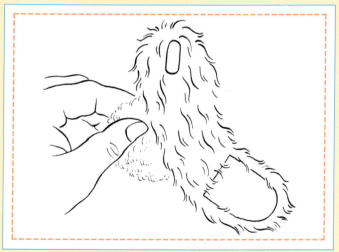

Step 7

6. Now the arm joints can be inserted – these will give the teddy bear the ability to move its arms when it is finished. Inside the arm, locate the mark that indicates the joint position and make a small hole at this point with your awl or knitting needle. Place the joint inside the arm and push the stem out through the hole. As the stems on these joints are much bigger than those on the eyes you may find that you will have to go back and make the hole slightly larger.

7. Once the joint is in place the arm can be softly stuffed with polyester filling. Put a little of the stuffing in the top of the arm, to hold the joint in place as you work, then add a little more to the paw pad area. Work from both ends until you get to the middle. Check carefully as you go along that there are no areas that have been missed or where the filling has become knotted up inside, as this will result in a very lumpy bear.

If there are any problems it is better to take all the filling out and start again – it will be worth it in the end.

8. When you are happy with the feel of the arm close the opening with ladder stitch.

9. Repeat the process with the other arm. Firstly attach the paw pad to the inner arm in the method shown on page 46. Make sure you match up points M and N on the straight edges of the inner arm and the paw pad and keep the straight edges level.

10. Unfold the paw pad and place it, right side in, against the corresponding outer arm, pinning into place. Line the fabric up carefully before you oversew it together, remembering to leave the opening for turning and stuffing. Stitch together, tucking in the pile as you go.

11. Add the joint to this arm, making the hole for the stem with an awl or knitting needle. Push the joint through from the inside of the arm and hold with some stuffing.

12. Stuff the arm from both ends until you reach the middle, making sure the stuffing is firm and evenly distributed. Close the opening with ladder stitch.

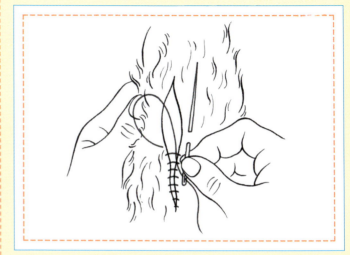

Step 8

Making the Bear

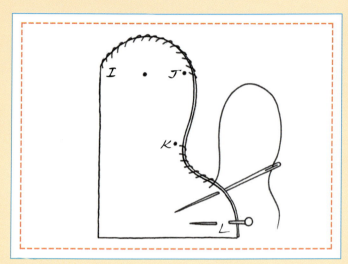

Step 1

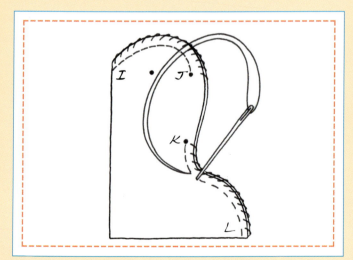

Step 2

Legs

The legs are constructed differently from the arms as there are only two pieces to bring together.

1. Take one of the leg pieces and fold it in half with right sides together. Pin carefully around the curved shape of the leg, making sure that the bottom straight edges are level. Oversew from point I to J and from point K to L, leaving the opening between points J and K clear, as marked on the pattern, for turning and stuffing. Also leave the bottom straight edge open for inserting the foot pad.

2. Remove the pins and stitch the leg from point I to J and then from point K to L, leaving the opening as marked on the pattern. Do not turn the leg right side out yet as the foot pad has to be inserted next.

3. Take one of the foot pads and position, with point L on the foot pad lining up with point L on the leg. Place a pin at this point to secure it, then place the next pin directly opposite the first one at the bottom of the foot pad.

4. Continue to pin around the foot pad using as many pins as necessary to hold the foot pad securely in place. Then oversew around the edge before removing the pins and stitching in place, following the seam allowance and outline of the foot pad very carefully in order to give a symmetrical finish.

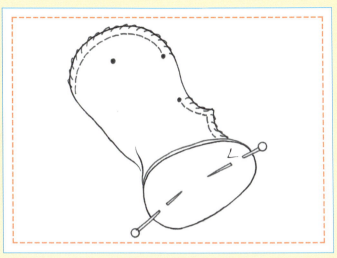

Step 3

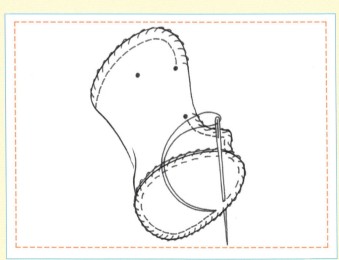

Step 4

Making the Bear

Step 5

Step 6

5. Turn the leg right side out and look inside to locate the mark for the joint position. Make a small hole here with your awl or knitting needle and place the joint inside the leg, pushing the shank out through the hole you have just made.

6. Now you can stuff the leg with the polyester stuffing, using the same method as you used for the arm. Start with some stuffing at the top of the leg to hold the joint in place as you work. Then move down to the foot pad and finally work up until you reach the middle. As you work, check carefully that there are no lumps and bumps in the leg, but also check that the foot pad is a nice, even and rounded shape.

7. When the leg has taken shape with enough stuffing, the opening can be closed with a double length of thread and a series of ladder stitches.

8. Repeat the process with the other leg: Fold the remaining leg piece in half, right sides together. Pin, oversew and then stitch from point I to J and from point K to L.

9. Position the footpad on the leg with point L on the pad corresponding to point L on the leg. Pin and then oversew around the edge. Then stitch into place, being careful to give a symmetrical finish.

10. With the leg turned right side out, make a small hole through at the joint position with an awl or knitting needle. Insert the joint and push the shank through.

11. Stuff the leg carefully, working from both ends until you meet in the middle. Ensure that you add the stuffing smoothly and evenly.

12. Close the opening of the leg with ladder stitch.

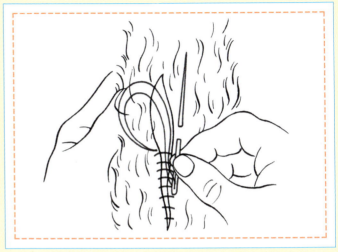

Step 12

Making the Bear

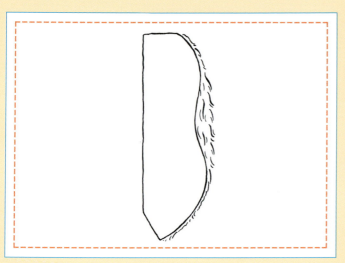

Step 1a

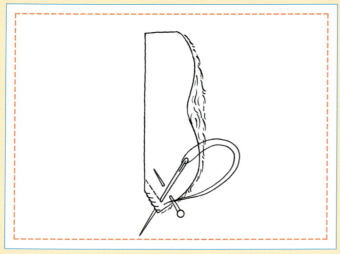

Step 1b

Body

This bear has a very simple body with just one dart at the base to give extra shape.

1. Before the body pieces can be joined together you must first make the darts at the bottom of each one. This is simply a matter of folding each body piece, right sides together, to bring the straight edges of the dart together (1a). Pin to hold in place, then oversew the edges of the dart, remove the pins and stitch (1b).

2. Place the body pieces right sides together, making sure that the straight edges at the top of the body are level and the seams of the darts are matching. Pin at these points first to stop the pieces from moving about, then add more pins around the edges of the body.

3. Oversew the edges of the pieces together, leaving the opening clear as marked on the pattern for turning and stuffing. Also keep the top straight edge open so that you can attach the head later.

Remove the pins and stitch from point E right around the front of the body to point F, then leave the gap for the opening and stitch from point G to H.

Remember to leave the top straight edge open ready to attach the head. Do not turn the body right side out yet, as this will make it more difficult to attach the head.

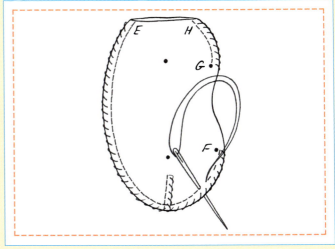

Step 3

Making the Bear

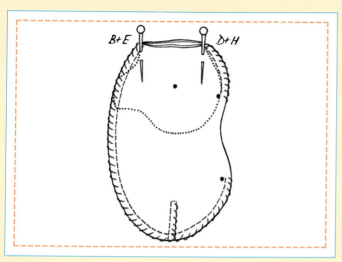

Step 1

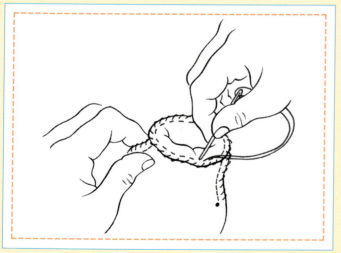

Step 2

Assembly

Now that all of the pieces are complete it is time to join them all together.

1. Start by stitching the head to the body. Place the head upside down inside the body so that the bottom straight edge of the head matches the top straight edge of the body, point B on the head matches point E on the body and point D on the head matches point H on the body.

Pin the head to the body at these points to hold it in the correct position while you continue to add more pins. With the head positioned like this the bear will look straight forward but if you prefer you can turn the head so that your bear will look either left or right.

2. Once the head has been pinned in place, oversew the edges together, then remove the pins and carefully stitch the head to the body. Check that the seam catches the fabric all the way around. This is a tricky area to manoeuvre a sewing machine so you may find it easier to sew the head on by hand.

3. Turn the body and head right side out ready to attach the arms and legs. Inside the body find the first arm position and use a sharp tool to make a small hole. Take one of the arms and push the shank of the joint through the hole in the body.

Check that the arm is facing forwards, with the paw pads closest to the body, as it is very easy to put the arms and legs on backwards!

4. From inside the body place the joint disc on the shank and secure the arm in place with the metal washer. Push the washer onto the shank, then check the arm to make sure that it can be moved. If it is too loose, push the washer further onto the shank but only far enough to stop the arm from feeling insecure.

If the joints are too tight the arm will not be able to be moved at all, so work carefully, only pushing the washer further onto the shank a little at a time and constantly check the tightness of the joint. Repeat this with the other arm and then with both legs (checking again that these are facing in the right direction before securing in place with the metal washers).

Step 3

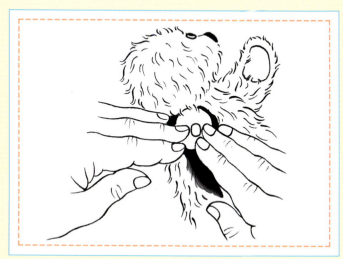
Step 4

Making the Bear

Step 5

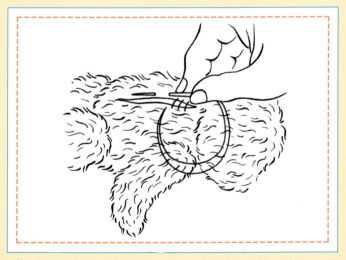

Step 6

5. With the limbs in place you can now add stuffing to the head. Add a little at a time, shaping as you go to give a rounded appearance. Check for lumps and hollows that may spoil the overall appearance of your bear. Once you are happy with the head then continue to add stuffing to the body. Gently mould the shape of the bear as you go, paying particular attention to the joint areas.

6. When you are happy with the firmness and shape of the bear, close the final seam with a double length of sewing thread and ladder stitch.

7. Finish by attaching the ears. Pin each of the ears to the head, trying different positions until you get a look that you are happy with. Different positions will change the character of your bear so do try various arrangements, making sure that the overall effect is symmetrical.

8. Once you have decided on the position for the ears, stitch them in place with a ladder stitch. Start at the top of the ear and work your way down the back edge, then continue up the front of the ear until you reach the top again.

Step 7

Step 8

61

Finishing Touches

Pulling the fur pile out of the seams

Brushing the fur

It is worth spending a little bit of time on a few finishing touches that will make all the difference to your bear.

During the sewing it is inevitable that some of the fur will get trapped in the seams. This can be freed with a needle or pin, which you use to gently pull the fur from the stitching. This will take a little time but it will help to hide the seam lines and give a generally 'fluffier' appearance.

Once all of the fur has been freed the bear will need an overall brush but be careful not to use a brush with bristles that are too stiff as this may damage the fur. Ideally a soft bristle brush should be used to gently tease the fur. If this is not available a comb should help to tidy up the pile.

Quite often you will find that some of the fur is hiding the eyes. However, trimming some of it away using a small pair of sharp, pointed scissors can rectify this. Follow the direction of the pile as you trim and be very careful if you choose to do this, as once the fur has been cut away it cannot be put back!

Finally, you can tie a brightly coloured ribbon around the neck of your bear to give him the perfect finish.

Although your teddy bear doesn't really need any more dressing than a simple ribbon, that doesn't mean you can't add more accessories if you wish. Remember, if you want to dress the bear up, try to use fabrics that will co-ordinate and contrast with the bear's natural colouring.

If the bear is to be male why not dress him in a fancy bowtie and colourful waistcoat. If the bear is to be female she could be dressed in a simple summer dress or skirt. Skirts are very easy to make and don't require very much material.

Alternatively, why not give your bear a profession by dressing it in a military cap, a policeman's helmet or even a teacher's mortarboard. Alternatively, a replica Christening gown would make an ideal outfit for a Christening gift.

You don't have to limit yourself to clothes either. If you so desire, you could add a badge, a bracelet or even a pair of earrings.

Tying the ribbon

Adding earrings

Conclusion

The finished bear

Now that you've made one teddy bear you may wish to make more.

If you want to take this wonderfully satisfying hobby further you will find that material is easy to come by. The colour of the fur will make a difference to the character of your bear as will the material you use for the eyes. It's up to you how many movable parts you want; you may prefer to create a teddy bear with stiff limbs.

You may want to keep your work to yourself. On the other hand teddy bears make terrific gifts for children – and adults. It is immensely gratifying to see the look of delight on a child's face when they first meet their new friend. What's more, the child may decide to keep your gift close at hand forever more.

You may be tempted to tell the child all about the hard work that went into creating the teddy, but why not make up a story instead, all about the teddy bear's adventures before he or she arrived to keep the child company?

Whatever you do, remember that teddy bear making – just like teddy bear owning – should always be fun.

Picture Credits
Key: Top – t; middle – m; bottom – b; left – l; right – r.
4: Topham Picture Point. 5: Corbis. 7-8: Topham Picture Point. 10: Topham Picture Point. 11: Allstar. 12: (t) Topham Picture Point. 13: (t) Bettman/Corbis. 15: Topham Picture Point. 23: (t) Action Press/Rex Features. 25: Topham Picture Point. 26: Christie's Images/Corbis. 29: (b) Topham Picture Point. 32: (t) Allstar. 33. Allstar. 34-35: Topham Picture Point.